The Illustrated
Parables of Jesus

Jean-François Kieffer
Christine Ponsard

Translated by Janet Chevrier

The Illustrated
Parables of Jesus

for Children

Ignatius

MAGNIFICAT.

To help us better understand him, Jesus often told stories, called "parables". They were drawn from the everyday life of the men and women around him. Indeed, we all know

that a lost sheep is a catastrophe for the shepherd,

that it takes a lot of care and patience from the gardener for a tree to bear fruit,

that a feast is very sad when the guests refuse to come,

that a child is unhappy when he feels alone and far from his father.

Everyone gathered around Jesus who heard these parables then understood a little better that God loved each one of them,

like the shepherd who went in search of the lost sheep,

like the gardener who watched over the budding fruit on his tree,

like the one who invited and welcomed to his feast all those who had not been on his guest list,

like the father who never stopped watching out for the return of his child.

Through these parables, Jesus shows you that you, too, are

that little sheep who sometimes strays from the flock and needs to hear the shepherd's call to find his way back to the fold,

that beautiful tree which will bear much fruit if you let the Lord love you,

that guest invited to the great feast where God wishes to gather all men,

that child who throws himself into his father's arms, asking his forgiveness.

TABLE OF CONTENTS

THE BIRDS AND THE FLOWERS

Matthew 6:25–34

We're going to need more money . . .

What are we going to eat tomorrow?

Don't be anxious . . .

Look at the birds in the sky . . .

They don't sow or reap grain to store in barns. Yet our heavenly Father feeds them!

And the lilies of the field! Look how beautiful they are: even King Solomon was never so beautifully clothed!

If God takes such good care of the wild flowers and the birds, will he not take even better care of you?

Don't worry about tomorrow: your Father looks after you.

Seek first the kingdom of God, and you will want for nothing!

A GOOD MEASURE

Luke 6:31 and 37–38

Jesus explains how to love . . .

Do to others as you would like to have them do to you!

Do not judge, and you will not be judged.

Do not condemn, and you will not be condemned.

Forgive, and you will be forgiven.

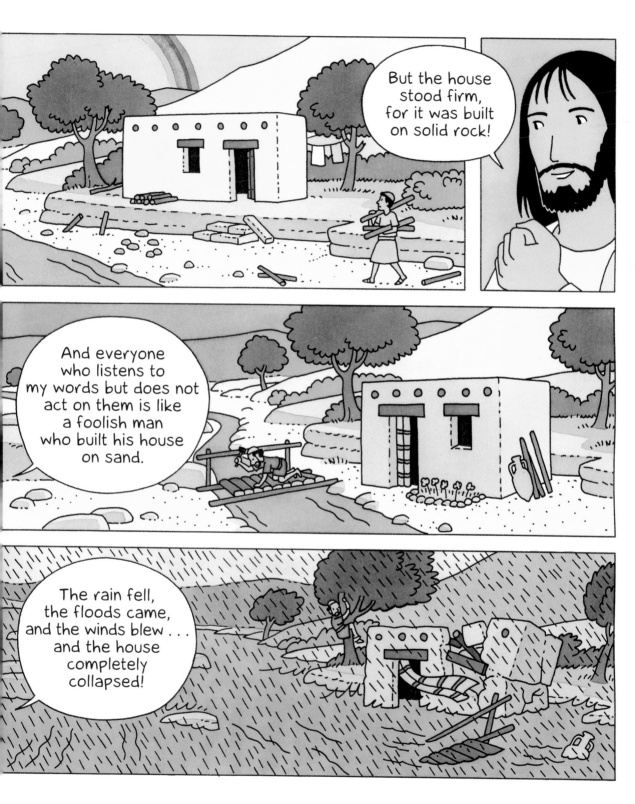

THE GOOD SEED AND THE WEEDS

Matthew 13:24–30

Jesus tells the crowd this parable:

The kingdom of heaven . . .

. . . is like a man who sows good seed in his field.

During the night, his enemy comes and sows weeds all through the wheat.

When the wheat begins to grow, the weeds appear as well.

Where have these weeds come from?

An enemy has done this!

Do you want us to pull them up?

No, you might uproot the wheat at the same time!

Let them grow together until the harvest. Then I will tell the harvesters:

"Pull up the weeds first and burn them!

Then reap the wheat and gather it into my barn."

THE TREASURE AND THE PEARL

Matthew 13:44–46

The kingdom of heaven is like a treasure hidden in a field.

A man finds the treasure.

He quickly hides it again.

He joyfully goes to sell all he owns and buys the field.

Again, the kingdom of heaven is like a pearl of great value.

A merchant sees this pearl . . .

He goes to sell all he has . . .

And he buys the pearl!

THE SEED THAT GROWS BY ITSELF

Mark 4:26–29

The kingdom of God may be compared to . . .

. . . a man who scatters seed in his field.

At night, he sleeps . . .

In the morning, he gets up . . .

And all this time, without his knowing how, the seed sprouts and grows.

The land produces first the blade, then the ear, then the grain of wheat.

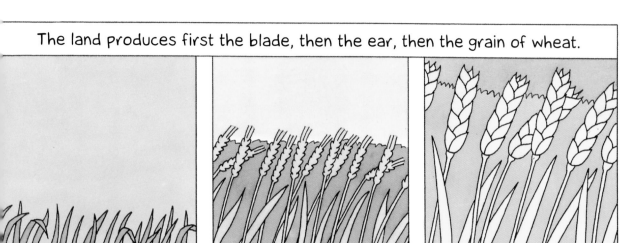

When the wheat is ripe, it's time for the harvest!

THE GOOD SAMARITAN

Luke 10:25–37

To try to trick Jesus, an expert of the law asks him a question:

Master, what must I do to have eternal life?

What is written in the law?

"You will love the Lord, your God, with all your heart, with all your soul, with all your strength, and with all your mind, and your neighbor as yourself."

That's correct. Do this, and you will have life!

And . . . who, then, is my neighbor?

So Jesus tells this parable:

A man was going down from Jerusalem to Jericho . . .

He came upon robbers, who stripped him and beat him before going off, leaving him half dead.

A priest going down this road saw him, crossed to the other side, and passed him by.

Then a Temple servant arrived, saw him, crossed to the other side, and passed him by.

But a Samaritan traveler arrived. He saw him and was moved with compassion.

He approached, poured oil and wine on his wounds, and bandaged them . . .

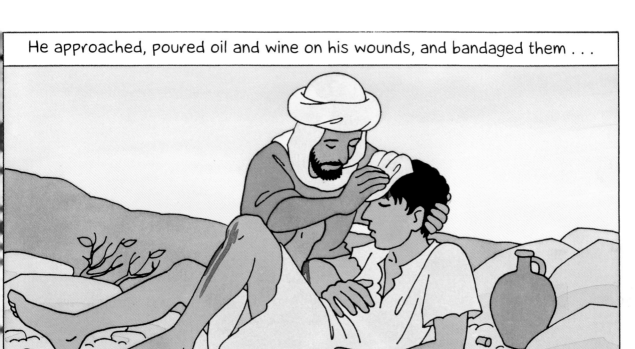

. . . Then he sat him on his donkey, led him to an inn, and took care of him.

The next day, he gave two coins to the innkeeper:

Take care of him, and if you spend more than this, I will repay you on my way back.

THE FIG TREE

Luke 13:6–9

To speak to us about God's patience, Jesus tells this parable:

A man has a fig tree planted in his orchard . . .

He comes to look for fruit . . .

For three years now, I've come looking for fruit on this fig tree and have found none!

It's using up the soil: cut it down!

Master, leave it for another year!

I'll hoe it and fertilize it . . .

Perhaps it will bear fruit in the future!

Hmm . . .

If not, you can cut it down . . .

THE LOST SHEEP

Luke 15:4–6

To help his friends understand how God forgives, Jesus tells them this story:

A shepherd has a hundred sheep . . .

If he loses one, he leaves the other ninety-nine to go look for the lost one.

When he finds it, he is overjoyed!

He returns, carrying it on his shoulders.

Then, he calls his neighbors:

Come rejoice with me, I've found my lost sheep!

THE PRODIGAL SON

Luke 15:11–32

Jesus speaks about the goodness of God, our Father:

A man has two sons . . .

The younger one asks for his inheritance.

Then he leaves for a faraway land . . .

. . . where he wastes all his money.

When he has nothing left, he gets a job taking care of pigs.

I'm starving! I'm going to return to my father's house and ask him to take me on as a hired worker.

So he sets off on his way home to his father.

His father spots him in the distance.

Father, I've sinned against heaven and against you. I don't deserve to be called your son!

But the father calls his servants.

Quick, bring him the finest robe!

Kill a fattened calf, and prepare a feast!

For my son was lost, but now he's been found!

And then the celebration begins.

When the older son comes home from work, he hears the music.

What's going on?

Your brother is back, and your father has killed a fattened calf!

Then the older brother becomes angry.

Come in, my child!

No! For I always obeyed you, and you never even gave me a little goat to feast on with my friends . . .

And when HE returns, after throwing away all your money, you kill a fattened calf for him!

My child, you are always with me, and everything I have is yours . . .

But I had to celebrate: your brother was lost and has now been found!

THE UNFORGIVING SERVANT

Matthew 18:21–35

Here is what Jesus tells us to teach us how to forgive:

A king wished to settle his accounts with his servants . . .

This one owes you a lot of money!

I don't have the money to pay you back . .

Then, I will sell all you own!

Be patient, I will pay you back!

Go! You owe me nothing anymore.

As he was leaving, the servant met a friend who owed him a little money.

Pay me back what you owe!

Be patient, I'll pay you back!

NO! You're going to prison!

His friends were very upset and went to tell all to the king. He had his servant called.

Wicked servant, why didn't you take pity on him as I took pity on you?

And he had him put in prison until he could pay back all he owed.

This is how my heavenly Father will treat you unless each of you forgives his brother with all his heart!

THE TWO SONS

Matthew 21:28–32

In the Jerusalem Temple, Jesus addresses the chief priests and the elders:

What do you think of this story? A man had two sons . . .

He went to the first one:

My son, go out and work in my vineyard!

No, I don't want to!

But later, the son repented and went to work.

The father went to his second son:

My son, go out and work in my vineyard!

Yes, Father, right away!

But he did not go!

Which of the two did his father's will?

The first one!

Then listen well: when John the Baptist came to you to ask you to repent, you didn't listen to him. Sinful people repented and changed. But despite that, you still did not repent . . .

THE PHARISEE AND THE TAX COLLECTOR

Luke 18:9–14

To those who are convinced they are righteous and look down on everyone else, Jesus tells this parable:

Two men go up to the Temple to pray . . .

One is a Pharisee, the other a tax collector.

The Pharisee stands up and prays to himself:

My God, I thank you that I am not like the others—greedy, dishonest, unfaithful—or even like this tax collector . . .

I fast twice a week, and I give a tenth of all I earn to charity . . .

The tax collector stands at a distance, not even daring to raise his eyes to heaven.

My God, have pity on me, a sinner!

It's the tax collector who is righteous, not the other . . .

He who exalts himself will be humbled; he who humbles himself will be exalted!

THE WEDDING GUESTS

Matthew 22:1–10

Jesus explains how God invites us into his kingdom:

A king is preparing a wedding feast for his son . . .

Quick, go get the guests!

The king invites you to his son's wedding!

No, I have to go work in my field!

The king invites you to his son's wedding!

I can't leave my business!

The king invites you . . .

Go away!

No one wanted to come! The feast is ready, but those who were invited were not worthy . . .

Go out and invite everyone you meet!

The servants go into the roads and gather everyone they find . . .

And the wedding hall is filled with guests!

THE TEN MAIDENS

Matthew 25:1–13

The kingdom of heaven is like ten maidens invited to a wedding . . .

They take their lamps to go welcome the bridegroom. Five take oil for their lamps; five forget to bring any.

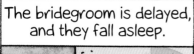
The bridegroom is delayed, and they fall asleep.

In the middle of the night:

It's the bridegroom! Go out to meet him!

Our lamps are going out . . .

Give us some of your oil!

There won't be enough for us and you . . . Go buy some instead!

While they run off, the bridegroom arrives . . .

The maidens who are ready go into the wedding hall with him, and the door is locked.

When the others come back . . .

Lord, let us in!

No, I do not know you!

Stay awake, for you know neither the day nor the hour!

THE TALENTS*

Matthew 25:14–30

Jesus does not like laziness!

Before leaving on a journey, a man entrusts his money to his servants . . .

They receive different amounts, each according to his ability.

One receives five talents; with them he earns five more.

Another receives two talents; with them he earns two more.

The third receives only one; he decides to bury it.

* Gold, silver, or copper coins used in trade

42

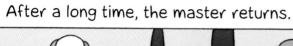
After a long time, the master returns.

You gave me five talents; here are five more!

Well done, good servant! Come, share your master's joy!

You gave me two talents; here are two more!

Well done, good servant! Come, share your master's joy!

I was afraid of you; I buried your money: here it is!

Bad, lazy servant!

"Take the talent from him, and give it to the one with ten! And throw him out!"

BE WATCHFUL!

Mark 13:33–37

A few days before dying, Jesus speaks about his return . . .

Be watchful! You do not know when the time will come.

Imagine a man who leaves on a journey . . .

He puts his servants in charge of his house and gives work to each of them.

He orders the gatekeeper to be on the watch.

You, too, be watchful: you don't know when the master will return.
In the evening or at midnight? At cockcrow* or in the morning?

He could arrive without warning
and find you sleeping!

*at dawn, at daybreak

THE TRUE VINE

John 15:1–8

Jesus explains to his disciples that they must remain united to him.

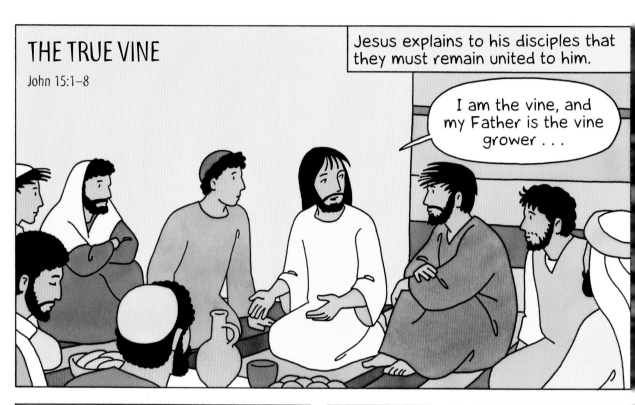

I am the vine, and my Father is the vine grower . . .

My Father takes away the branches that bear no fruit.

Those that do, he prunes, so that they bear even more fruit.

I am the vine . . .

. . . and you are the branches.

A branch cannot bear fruit unless it remains on the vine! Neither can you, unless you remain in me.

If you remain in me, if you keep my words, whatever you ask will be done for you.

My Father is glorified when you bear much fruit!

Original French edition:
Les Paraboles de Jésus en bandes dessinées

© 2002 by Groupe Fleurus-Mame, Paris
© 2011 by Ignatius Press, San Francisco • Magnificat USA LLC, New York
All rights reserved.
ISBN Ignatius Press 978-1-58617-649-5 • ISBN Magnificat 978-1-936260-25-6

Printed by Tien Wah Press, Malaysia
Printed on June 15, 2011
Job Number MGN 11007
Printed in Malaysia in compliance with the Consumer Protection Safety Act, 2008.